No Woman No Cr
Page 6
I Shot The Sheril...
Page 10
Exodus.
Page 13
Jamming.
Page 16
Is This Love?
Page 20
Lively Up Yourself.
Page 25
Could You Be Loved?
Page 30
Waiting In Vain.
Page 37
Roots Rock Reggae.
Page 42
Three Little Birds.
Page 46

Robert Nesta Marley.
1945-1981
Ten Greatest Hits.

Wise Publications
London/New York/Sydney/Cologne
Exclusive distributors:
Music Sales Limited
8/9 Frith Street, London W1V 5TZ, England.
Music Sales Pty. Limited
120 Rothschild Avenue, Rosebery, NSW 2018, Australia.

Book design by Pearce Marchbank.

"If God hadn't given me a song to sing, I wouldn't have a song to sing."

This book © copyright 1981 by Wise Publications
ISBN 0.86001.966.7.
Order No. AM 29539

Unauthorised reproduction of any part of this publication by any means including photocopying is an infringement of copyright.

Printed in England by: Halstan & Co. Ltd., Amersham, Bucks.

"Bob Marley was the one man who raised black consciousness among the youth of our generation. He helped us understand a little better the problems that blacks around the world are faced with today...His effect on our lives will remain with us forever."
Bob Geldof.

"I'm a rebel, soul rebel. I'm a capturer, soul adventurer."

"Bob Marley was Jamaica's greatest artist and it's very, very sad to lose him this way."
Eddy Grant.

"He became a cultural ambassador for Jamaica, expressing the need for unity among peoples of different colour, tongues and creed.... His spirit will always live on in his music...."
The Hon. Edward Seaga,
Prime Minister of Jamaica.

"Wake up and live."

"The Devil always come in between
politicians and they start quarrelling.
Y'have to imagine what really go on,
because power became a pride
business instead of we live together
and trade together and stop the war."

"When the race is hard to run, and you just can't stand the pace/All I know is that Jah will be waiting there/I know."
from "I Know."

"If politics deal with prophecy, then good. If it deal with sommat else, then it no good. Now is a wicked time, but wickedness come to a perpetual end. Prophecy a fulfil."

"Everything that God said in prophecies have to come true. It's just that some people are more aware of it, more aware of the spiritual part of life."

No Woman No Cry.

Words and music by Vincent Ford

© Copyright 1975 Tuff Gong Music, USA. Rights throughout the World
(excluding the Caribbean) controlled by Almo Music Corp., U.S.A.
Rondor Music (London) Ltd., 10a Parsons Green, London SW6 for the
British Commonwealth (except Canada, Australia, New Zealand and the
British Far East Territories), Eire and Czechoslovakia.

To Coda ⊕

no cry
don't shed no tears   1.2.3. No wo - man, no cry _____   said, said,
don't shed no tears _____

Am   F   C   F   C   G

said I re-mem-ber when we used _ to sit _____   in the government yard in

C   G   Am   F   C   G

Trench-town,   Ob - er - ob - er- serv - ing the
and then Geor - gie would

Am   F   C   G

hy - po- crites,   as they would   min - gle with the good peo - ple we
make the fi - re light,   as it was   log wood burn - ing through the

Am   F   C   G

7

I Shot The Sheriff.

Words and music by Bob Marley

© Copyright 1973 Cayman Music Inc., USA.
Administered by Leosong Copyright Service Ltd., 7–8 Greenland Place, London NW1, for the British Commonwealth
(except Canada, Australasia, Singapore and Hong Kong) and Eire.

Moderately slow 2-beat

E♭
3 fr.
Dm
Gm
3 fr.
kill - ing of a dep - u - ty. For the
kill it be - fore it grow. He said
aim - ing to shoot me down. So I
day the bot - tom will drop out. Yes, one
E♭
3 fr.
Dm7
Gm
life of a dep - u - ty.
kill it be - fore it grow.
shot, I shot him down.
day the bot - tom will drop out.
But I say:
f
1. 2. 3.
4.
D. C. (Lyric I) and fade

Exodus.

Words and music by Bob Marley

© Copyright 1977 Bob Marley Music Ltd., controlled for USA & Canada by
Almo Music Corp., rest of the World (excluding Caribbean) by
Rondor Music Inc., Rondor Music (London) Ltd., 10a Parsons Green,
London SW6 for the United Kingdom and Eire.

14

Jamming.

Words and music by Bob Marley

© Copyright 1977 Bob Marley Music Ltd., controlled for USA & Canada by
Almo Music Corp., rest of the World (excluding Caribbean) by
Rondor Music Inc., Rondor Music (London) Ltd., 10a Parsons Green,
London SW6 for the United Kingdom and Eire.

17

We're jam-ming___ jam-ming___ jam-ming___ jam-ming we're

F#m7   Bm   E7

jam-ming right straight from Jah.___ Ho - ly mount:

G   F#m7   Bm

___ Zi - on   Ho - ly mount___ Zi - on

Em   Bm   Em

Jah sit - teth in Mount Zi - on   and rules___ all

Bm   Bm

Is This Love?

Words and music by Bob Marley

© Copyright 1978 Bob Marley Music Ltd., controlled for USA & Canada by
Almo Music Corp., rest of the World (excluding Caribbean) by
Rondor Music Inc., Rondor Music (London) Ltd., 10a Parsons Green,
London SW6 for the United Kingdom and Eire.

23

Lively Up Yourself.

Words and music by Bob Marley

© Copyright 1973 Cayman Music Inc., USA. Administered by Leosong
Copyright Service Ltd., 7–8 Greenland Place, London NW1, for the
British Commonwealth (except Canada, Australasia, Singapore and
Hong Kong) and Eire.

be a - live to day ___ You're gon - na

live-ly up your - self ___ and don't say no ___ You

live-ly up your self ___ big Dad - dy says so ___

You live-ly up your - self ___ and don't be no drag

Additional Lyrics.

What you got that I don't know,
I'm a trying to wonder why you act so
(Hey do you hear what the man say?)
Lively up your woman in the morning
Time you'll
Keep a lively up your woman when
The evening comes
And take her take ya.

You rock so you rock so
You dip so you dip so
You skank so you skank so and don't
Be no drag
You come so you come so for reggae is
Be no drag
Get what you got in that bag
What have you got in the other bag you
Got hanging there?
What you say you got?
I don't believe you.

Could You Be Loved?

Words and music by Bob Marley

© Copyright 1980 Bob Marley Music Ltd., controlled for USA & Canada by
Almo Music Corp., rest of the World (excluding Caribbean) by
Rondor Music Inc., Rondor Music (London) Ltd., 10a Parsons Green,
London SW6 for the United Kingdom and Eire.

and be loved?

Don't let them fool you

Or ev - en try to school you.

Oh no

We've got a mind of our own So

go to hell—— if what you're think— ing is not right——

Love would nev-er leave—us a - lone.—— In the dark - ness— there

must come out—— the light.——— Could you be loved—

———————————— and be loved?———

—— Could you be loved———

Don't let them change you

Or ev - en re - ar -

- range you.———— Oh, no!————

We've got a life—— to live——

They say———————— on - ly,——

34

Waiting In Vain.

Words and music by Bob Marley

©Copyright 1977 Bob Marley Music Ltd., controlled for USA & Canada by
Almo Music Corp., rest of the World (excluding Caribbean) by
Rondor Music Inc., Rondor Music (London) Ltd., 10a Parsons Green,
London SW6 for the United Kingdom and Eire.

know when you're gon - na come___ see,
I'm wait-ing for my turn.

Cmaj7

CHORUS

I don't wan - na wait__ in vain___ for your_ love;__

Gmaj7   Cmaj7

I don't wan - na wait__ in vain___ for your_ love;__

Gmaj7   Cmaj7

To Coda ⊕

I don't wan - na wait___ in vain___ for your_ love.__

Gmaj7   Cmaj7

40

'Cos_____ sum - mer is____ here,___ I'm still wait - ing__

C D Bm Am

there.___ Win - ter is____ here___ and I'm still wait - ing

C D Bm Am

D. S. al Coda ✛ **CODA**

there._____

Oh I don't wan-na I don't wan-na

Cmaj7 Gmaj9

Repeat to fade

I don't wan-na I don't wan-na I don't wan-na wait in vain.____ No___

Cmaj7

Roots Rock Reggae.

Words and music by Vincent Ford

© Copyright 1976 Tuff Gong Music, USA. Rights throughout the World
(excluding the Caribbean) controlled by Almo Music Corp., U.S.A.
Rondor Music (London) Ltd., 10a Parsons Green, London SW6 for the
British Commonwealth (except Canada, Australia, New Zealand and the
British Far East Territories), Eire and Czechoslovakia.

Roots, rock, reg - gae. ___ This a reg - gae mu - sic.

Hey mis - ter mu - sic, ___

sure sound good to me. ___ I can't re - fuse ___

___ it, ___ what to be, got to be. ___

43

Feel like danc - in', _____ dance 'cause we are free. _____

_____ Feel like danc - in', _____

come dance with me. _____ Roots, rock, _ reg - gae. _

(Repeat 2 times)

_____ This a reg - gae mu - sic.

44

Three Little Birds.

Words and music by Bob Marley

© Copyright 1977 Bob Marley Music Ltd., controlled for USA & Canada by
Almo Music Corp., rest of the World (excluding Caribbean) by
Rondor Music Inc., Rondor Music (London) Ltd., 10a Parsons Green,
London SW6 for the United Kingdom and Eire.

9/91 (12462)